Invocations and Prayers of Khwaja Abdullah Ansari of Herat

Translations by
Sardar Sir Jogendra Singh and
Arthur John Arberry

Introduction by
Syeda Saiyidain Hameed

SPEAKING
TIGER

SPEAKING TIGER BOOKS LLP
125A, Ground Floor, Shahpur Jat,
Near Asiad Village, New Delhi - 110 049

First published by Speaking Tiger Books 2022

ISBN: 978-93-5447-212-1
eISBN: 978-93-5447-220-6

10 9 8 7 6 5 4 3 2 1

Typeset in Adobe Caslon Pro by Jojy Philip
Printed at HT Media Ltd, Greater Noida

Sheikh Khwaja Abdullah Ansari (1006–1086 CE) was born in Herat, Afghanistan. Ansari excelled in the knowledge of Hadith, history and law. He became a revered authority on Islamic mysticism and philosophy quite early in life and shared his wisdom with common people. His writings and collected sayings, in Persian and Arabic, continue to inspire Sufis and seekers around the world today. Khwaja Ansari's tomb – the shrine in Gazur Gah – is a pilgrimage site that attracts thousands every year.

Sardar Sir Jogendra Singh (1877–1946) was a scholar and statesman, born at Aira Estate in Kheri district of what used to be the United Provinces. He was a member of the Viceroy's Executive Council in India and served as Chairman of the Department of Health, Education and Lands. His *The Persian Mystics*, published by John Murray, London, in October 1939, is a rendering into English of the sayings of the mystic Abdullah Ansari of Herat. Singh was knighted in 1929 and co-founded the Khalsa National Party in 1936.

Arthur John Arberry (1905–1969) was a British scholar of Arabic literature, Persian studies, and Islamic studies. Arberry served as Head of Department of Classics at Cairo University in Egypt and is notable for introducing Rumi's work to the West through his selective translations. His English translation of the Qur'an, *The Koran Interpreted*, is popular amongst academics worldwide.

Syeda Saiyidain Hameed is a former Member of the Planning Commission of India and former Member of the National Commission for Women. She is a feminist and writer, who is widely recognized for her passionate engagement in public affairs and social issues, especially for women, minorities and peace. She is the Founder Member of the Muslim Women's Forum and a Founder Trustee of the Women's Initiative for Peace in South Asia. Hameed was awarded the Padma Shri in 2007.

CONTENTS

INTRODUCTION

MUNAJAT OF KHWAJA ABDULLAH PIR-I-HERAT

It is the time of tahajjud (pre-dawn prayer) when I have begun writing this.

I close my eyes and open the *Qur'an* to guide me in this mission. Miraculously, it opens on Surah An-Nisa, Ayat 95. I become aware then that an invisible hand had guided me to the Surah—which for many years has become my life's mission—Surah An-Nisa (The Women).

Ayat 95 states:

> *Those who stay at home—except those with valid excuses—are not equal to those who strive in the cause of Allah with their wealth and their lives.*
> *Allah has elevated in rank those who strive with their wealth and their lives above those who stay behind.*

All my life I have been a believer and I try to strive and fight for His cause—the cause of justice and love. My fight is for Islam which has become the most misunderstood religion in the world, for which I believe we Muslims are responsible. Islam has answers for us. This is why I may have been chosen to bring back from oblivion this gift for our highly troubled and deeply hurt world. Khwaja Abdullah Pir-i-Herat's prayers and supplications are presented here as the healing hand of a Sufi Pir who spoke of surrender and love over a 1000 years ago.

Thirty years ago, I found a copy of these Munajat (prayers), penned by Khwaja Abdullah, in the India Office Library (IOL) in London. I was not looking for them. I was conducting research on Maulana Abul Kalam Azad. My cousin Yasoob Hashmi, who had brought me there, and I were thrilled to discover our ancestor listed in the catalogue. The copy with the IOL stamp has lain with me three decades.

I may never have embarked on this mission if the editor and publisher Ravi Singh had not inspired me. Again, it was providence that he came to my home and offered to publish this work. Speaking Tiger is a publishing house which, to my thinking, was destined for this. I thought of my Maula Ali, the fourth Khalifa of Islam, who was called Sher-e-Yazdan, meaning Tiger of Allah. Need I say more?

Let me start with my beginning.

My lineage is narrated in *Shahnama-e-Islam*, a long poetic narration of the history of Islam, by the poet Hafeez Jalandhari. Here is the scene. It is the seventh century of the Christian calendar. The Prophet performs Hijrat from Mecca to Medina. He enters the city. People throng to welcome him. Everyone wants to host him. He leaves his destination unto his camel. 'I will stay where my camel stops', he announces. His camel stops before the house of

Abu Ayyub Ansari—the ancestor of the author of this book of prayer. The Prophet addresses the crowd, 'I will stay here, where my camel has sat down'.

Sahaba se kaha jab tak na ho masjid ki tayyari
Hamare mezbaan honge Abu Ayyub Ansari
Falak ne rashk se dekha us Ansari ki qismat ko
Abu Ayyub ghar mein le gaye saamaan e rehmat ko

He told his companions 'until the mosque is laid
Our host will be Abu Ayyub Ansari'
The skies looked with envy at kismet of Ansari
He ushered Allah's blessing into his humble home.

Abu Ismail Abdullah ibn Mohammad al-Ansari was born in Quhandiz, in the Persian province of Herat in 396 AH*. His ancestor, Abu Ayyub Ansari, was an 'ansar', or 'friend'—an appellation given to all citizens of Medina by virtue of their hospitality to the Prophet, hence Abdullah, too, was an Ansari. He was born on a Friday evening, on the 2nd of Shaban,† 396 AH (1006 CE). As he himself said, 'I am a springster. I was born in springtime and I dearly love the spring'. He learnt to write at the age of nine, and at fourteen he began to compose verses. In basic principles (usul), he followed Imam Ahmad Bin Khalil, a lexicographer, born in the year 718 CE in Oman. In subsidiary principles (forua),

---

* 'Year of the Hijrah'; Latin: *Anno Hegirae*

† The eight month in the Islamic calendar

he followed Imam Shafei, born in 767 CE in Gaza. Given his genius he could have become a theologian but he turned to Tasawwuf (Islamic mysticism or Sufism) under the tutelage of Sufi Abul al-Hasan al-Kharraqani (963-1033 CE) who claimed a deep spiritual relationship with Persian Sufi Bayazid Bastami.

Khwaja Abdullah is said to have suffered the fate of all geniuses and was exiled due to court jealousies as a consequence of his growing spiritual influence. But he was brought back with honour by the governor Nizam-al-Mulk Tusi, a Persian scholar, political philosopher and vizier of the Seljuk empire. Soon after he returned on Friday, 22nd Dhul Hijja* 481 AH (1086 CE), he 'attained visaal', which is the Sufi term for death. He is buried in Gazur Gah in Herat. His mausoleum became a highly revered Sufi pilgrimage. Common people believe in his miracles. Every day, especially every Friday night, many Dervishes stand in a circle in the precinct of his tomb and pray.

The man was a genius. It is recorded that as a child he had learnt about 100,000 Persian verses by heart. At the age of fourteen he had composed 6000 Arabic verses. More than thirty-two books in Persian and Arabic are attributed to him. Four of his best loved books are *Risala Munajat* (The Book of Prayer) *Tabqat-ul-Sufia* (Book of Sufis), *Zald-ul-Arfin* (Book of Saints) and *Kitab-i-Israr* (The Book of Mysteries).

His devoted disciples were from all over greater Iran and his society came to be known as Silsila-i-Ansari.

---

* The twelfth month in the Islamic calendar

The *Risala Munajat* is regarded among the most famous and popular works in Persian mystical literature.

Abdullah Ansari's descendant, Merak Shah, Badshah-e-Herat, was a patron of scholars. His son Khwaja Malik Ali travelled to India with his two sons Khwaja Masud and Khwaja Naseer. Begum Saliha Abid Hussain in her book on Maulana Hali writes that 'for some reason', leaving behind his pomp and splendour, Abdullah Ansari travelled all the way to India. That was the time of Sultan Ghiyas-ud-din Balban, who welcomed them to his kingdom. The Sultan's respect for them as scholars and teachers was reflected in giving them lands and honours in a very fertile part of his kingdom, Panipat, which would allow them to engage in their spiritual pursuits. People of this unique city excelled in the art of recitation of the *Qur'an*, called quirrat. In Panipat at the time, the most renowned Sufi was Bu Ali Shah Qalandar. Khwaja Malik Ali settled there in the year 1276.

Six hundred years later was born in his lineage the most illustrious descendant, known to the world as Khwaja Altaf Husain Hali. I was born almost a century later; he was my paternal grandmother's paternal grandfather. There are two reasons why Hali became a household word not only for Muslims but all Urdu-knowing Indians (a definition that cuts across religious divide) then, and should be widely known and read now. First that he spoke about Hindu-Muslim unity and second because he was not only a reformist but also the first feminist poet of India.

I visited Kabul in 2007, my one and only visit to my ancestral land. Despite many requests, I was not permitted to go to Herat to visit my ancestor's mausoleum where thousands of devotees throng every day. I was told it was not safe. Zalmai Rassoul, Advisor to President Hamid Karzai, presented me with a book about the mausoleums of Herat. And finally, I saw in those beautiful photographs, the place where he has lain for a thousand years. People in the photos are seen offering prayers and supplications. Today as I write this, I feel I have his benediction.

There are two persons who brought this work out of oblivion. First, Sardar Sir Jogendra Singh and second, father of our nation, Mohandas Karamchand Gandhi.

In the Foreword (Part One)—dated April 4, 1938—Mahatma Gandhi writes what is the compelling reason why this book must be read. He recommends it not only in the subcontinent but all across the world; to people of all faiths, all walks of life, all disciplines:

> *Islam has given the world mystics no less than Hinduism and Christianity. In this time when irreligion masquerades as religion, it is well to remind ourselves of what the best mind of all religions has thought and said. We must not like the frog in the well, who imagines the world ends with the wall surrounding his well, think that our religion alone represents the whole Truth and all others are false.*

Sardar Sir Jogendra Singh—the man to who I owe this treasure—was a scholar, linguist, public intellectual and statesman. His erudition and command of Persian language and Sufi philosophy left me with a sense of my own inadequacy to be writing about this intellectual giant.

I spoke to his grandson, Sardar Rupinder Singh, who verified what is available in the records. I learnt about his missal (clan) from his nephew, my friend Jagdeep Mann. He served on the Viceroy's Council, held army commission, headed several Sikh organizations but was foremost a scholar. Among his books on Sikhism, the title that struck me was *Thus Spake Guru Nanak*. His *Persian Mystics: Ansari* was published by John Murray, London, in October 1939. It went into fourteen editions between 1939 and 1959.

Arthur John Arberry, born in Portsmouth UK, was among the best scholars of Persian, Arabic and many other languages. He is best known for his translation and interpretation of the *Qur'an—The Holy Koran Interpreted*. His book *Sufism: An Account of Mystics of Islam* (1950) contains translations of Khwaja Abdullah Ansari's Prayers and Counsels.

This book, *Invocations and Prayers of Khwaja Abdullah Ansari of Herat*, is divided into two parts. The first part contains translations from the book *The Persian Mystics: Ansari* by Sardar Sir Jogendra Singh. Three sets of translations of prayers and invocations follow.

The second part contains the Nasa'ih, meaning pious counsels, translated by Arthur John Arberry. There is a short section of proverbs, and some verse extracts follow thereafter.

I have been reading these books over many years. For those who will open it now, I can promise it holds many answers to the problems that are overwhelming their fast-shrinking world and the growing distances with their loved ones. In case we become too despondent about the various afflictions that have gripped us since the turn of the century, whether it is the degraded environment, the massive disease or the mind-blowing virtual world, the Master has assured us:

'The world is a mere crossing
And not an abiding city of delight'

In his preface, Sardar Sir Jogendra Singh opens the garden door but does not take us by hand. He explains why he withdraws in favour of the Master's word:

I would rather let Ansari speak, than overload what he has so simply and directly said with comments of my own, from the shadows of a mind that lacks crystal clearness. I am confident that those who are on the mystic path of discovery will find in his sayings food for the soul.

My temptation, however, is to highlight some of his poetic prayers, which I justify by the fact that he is my ancestor. His spirit hovers over me as I highlight a few thoughts which I know are the need of the young and not so young to come to terms with their journey through these times. In a verse he describes the last words of Mansur Hallaj—a Persian mystic, a poet and Sufi teacher. For saying *Anal Haq (I am Truth)* he was sent to the gallows by the ruler. Here is the lesson Mansur imparts to his friend Shibli when he visits him as he is facing death:

When Mansur was imprisoned
For proclaiming oneness with God,
His friend Shibli asked him
'What is this love?'

'Come to-morrow
For answer,' he said.
Shibli obeyed and found Mansur
Facing the gallows.

Mansur looked at him
And said, 'Read the answer:
Love begins in absorbing the "I"
And ends thus':

'Its noose tightens
To squeeze out the self
Then comes the test of the Cross.
Stay if thou apprehendest the secret, otherwise go.'

I end my introduction with Abdullah Ansari's verse which explains The Divine Design; we may not understand it because of our human limitations. He gives an example of Prophet Abraham, the holiest of Allah's servants who came from the pagan 'idol shrine' and Abu Jehl, the 'unholiest' (he was the Prophet's sworn enemy) who came from the holiest place, Kaaba (Ka'bah):

O God Abu Jahl from the Ka'bah comes, Abraham from the idol shrine:
Thy Providence doth order all things;
What remains is but a vain pretence
O God there is indeed light in obedience
But the ruling of affairs is in thy providence

I have learnt about myself through the wisdom of this Old Man of Herat. I offer that humble knowledge to the reader. Otherwise, we will live our lives without once asking the question, 'who am I?' Thus the quol of Imam Ali is for all people, for all times:

Man Arafa Nafsahu
Faqad Arafa Rabbahu

When I recognized myself
I recognized my Rabb [God].

Syeda Saiyidain Hameed
January 2022

I am intoxicated with love of Thee
And need no fermented wine.
I am Thy bird
Free from need of seed
And safe from the snare of the fowler.
In the Ka'bah and in the Temple
Thou art the object of my search.
Else I am freed
From both these places of worship

—Khwaja Abdullah Ansari of Herat

PART ONE

THE PERSIAN MYSTICS: THE INVOCATIONS OF SHEIKH ABDULLAH ANSARI OF HERAT

Translated by

Sardar Sir Jogendra Singh

FOREWORD

Sardar Sir Jogendra Singh is to be congratulated on having given us his rendering into English of the Sayings of the Mystic Abdullah Ansari. Islam has given the world mystics no less than Hinduism or Christianity. In these days when irreligion masquerades as religion, it is well to remind ourselves of what the best mind of all the religions of the world has thought and said. We must not, like the frog in the well, who imagines that the universe ends with the wall surrounding his well, think that our religion alone represents the whole Truth and all the others are false. A reverent study of the other religions of the world would show that they are equally true as our own, though all are necessarily imperfect.

M. K. Gandhi

PREFACE

My friend Raja Sir Daljeet Singh handed over to me one day the sayings, in Persian, of Abdullah Ansari. He had discovered and treasured them, and now he offered to share his treasure with me. It was a real gift, for which I am deeply grateful.

I feel that these sayings contain true advice to guide the Pilgrim along the path of discipleship to the Temple of Peace. They come from the heart of a man who himself had trodden the path and found what his heart desired.

Abdullah Ansari had seen and experienced what is hidden from other eyes. His discovery proved that Truth is unchanging and that those who find it, in all ages and in all times, speak with unchallenged unanimity. They do not argue, but affirm, that anyone who is in earnest can lift the veil and resolve for himself the mysteries of life. Abdullah Ansari does not expound or explain, he simply states facts. His facts however are not within the cognition of those whose consciousness has not been freed from the clouding of the senses.

It is held that when a Seeker gives his heart and mind to the search, and disperses the mists that arise from tumultuous passions, Truth becomes brighter and brighter and fills the Soul with its light.

It is asserted that while reason is puzzling itself about mystery of consciousness, time and space, the man of Faith is going forward from discovery to discovery, in the growing illumination of his heart.

But it must be recognized that this knowledge is only available to those whose eyes are fixed, like an archer on the arrow and the object at which he aims, and that without purity of purpose and unceasing effort deliverance cannot be obtained.

In all ages and in all times men have sought and found truth. They have shown the way and means of attainment. But men have listened to the message with incredulity and continued the mad pursuit of sense objects.

Passions of body and mind govern men and kindle fires of desire, of greed, attachment, egoism and anger. These enslave and obscure the mind which must be freed, and restored to its pristine purity to reflect truth. The seekers of truth, therefore, concentrate all the strength in drawing away the mind from sense objects and to set it free from the dominations of fear and hate. Some follow the path of knowledge, and others the path of devotion, hoping to lose all sense of duality in the supreme uprising of love.

The world-forsakers are something of an enigma to world-seekers. The truth is that a Yogi or a Sufi gives up that which has no real value. He says that the bewildering fascination of the world is like the thirst of a deer in a desert, which drives it to follow shadows of a mirage, phantoms of water and trees and mocking cities that vanish when approached. According to him:

'What is its joy, what is its woe
But scented ash, that used to glow?
A sandal wood of long ago.
A camphor of the past.'

These God-filled men carry an aroma of sweetness and peace; of radiant joy and absolute serenity, in a restless world, having drunk from the source of life itself. The Ego no more drives them.

Mystics declare life to be a journey over an unknown path which is as straight and narrow as a razor. There is no other light but that of faith to guide the seeker, no sustenance but devotion. The track ahead cannot be seen. Going is uncertain, and pitfalls await the unwary. The seeker must travel in the dark. He must not cry for a candle to grope in the gloom or seek the rush-light of reason. He must go steadily forward, in the hope of reaching a great illumination, which awaits him at the journey's end.

There is no religion which has been without its mystics, men who, by their devotion, have unravelled the mystery of life and found God. They have spoken with no uncertain voice of the Truth that has been revealed to them.

It would profit little to dwell on the system of Sufism. Volumes have been written in Persian and other languages on the subject. It is not a system really. It is a way of life. It is beyond the range of reason. It cannot be comprehended, but it can be realized.

I would rather let Ansari speak, than overload what he has so simply and directly said with comments of my own, from the shadows of a mind that lacks crystal clearness. I am confident that those who are on the mystic path of discovery will find in his sayings food for the soul.

A great mystic has said:

> 'To know the world, is to despise it,
> To know God, is to be lost in His love.'

It seems that in all ages and in all times there come true teachers, who bear witness to the truths of religion, who speak of what they know, and are ready to share their knowledge with those who are prepared to follow the path of discipleship. The learned and the wise, the priesthood of all creeds, cannot reconcile itself to the direct methods of attainment of the mystics. The learned call these knowers *mystics,* because they cannot bring within the ambit of intellect what is beyond the bounds of intellect; the worldly wise in pursuit of their ambitions suspect their sanity, for they discard what they value most, according to them they preach the giving up of substances for a shadow. The priesthood with whom adherence to fixed ritual replaces the spirit of religion are afraid of their influence, and therefore, these devotees of God, sane, in an insane world, are only understood by those who are ready to follow truth.

The mystics pass like shooting stars, giving light to those who are ready to receive it, and disturbing others, who close their eyes, lest they may be dazzled by its brilliance. Generally the crowd drives them to the cross and the gallows, but Abdullah Ansari seems to have escaped both. Evidently he did not violate rules of rigid orthodoxy and led a life of sweetness, without compromising the truth, that was his, and which is enshrined in his teachings.

Life, for rich and poor alike, is full of joys and sorrows, as long as the ego drives and seeks satisfaction in things outside itself. It is a life of ambition, or pleasures of senses, or rivalries, or quest for power, for money, which even when gathered remains sterilized. For he who hoards money, deprives himself of its service. It is only when sickness of the soul grows and fatal fascination turn of the world fades, that true desire takes birth in the heart and the awakened self seeks the path of salvation.

It is said that an ancestor of Abdullah Ansari was in the Court of the prophet of Islam, in charge of his horses; and later came to Herat with Asaf, son of Kais. His father, Abu Mansur Mohammad Ansari, became a permanent resident of Herat.

Abdullah Ansari was born on Friday at sunset 396 Hijri or CE 1005. At the age of nine he displayed a remarkable mastery, and seemed to know all that was known on religion and philosophy; at the age of fourteen he sat in the company of the learned and discoursed wisely on all the subjects that were under discussion. Very wonderful are the powers that a soul brings with it, its garnered harvest of aeons of experience. Abdullah Ansari was born with knowledge. He had not to seek and discover it anew. He was an octogenarian when he departed from this earth. It is said that he had about a hundred thousand Persian verses by heart, and himself composed 6,000 verses in Arabic. There are four books in Persian which are still studied with reverence. These are

Risala Munajat—The Book of Prayer, *Tabqat-ul-Sufia*—The Book of Sufees, *Zald-ul-Arfin*—The Book of Saints, *Kitab-i-Israr*—The Book of Mysteries.

He gathered round him a band of devoted disciples, and this society came to be known as Silsila-i-Ansari, and is said to have survived up to the present time.

The following verses describe his soul's journey from material manifestation to spiritual absorption—

> 'From the unmanifest I came,
> And pitched my tent
> In the Forest of Material existence,
> I passed through
> Mineral and vegetable kingdoms,
> Then my mental equipment
> Carried me into the animal kingdom;
> Having reached there I crossed beyond it;
> Then in the crystal clear shell of human heart
> I nursed the drop of self into a Pearl,
> And in association with good men
> Wandered round the Prayer House,
> And having experienced that, crossed beyond it;
> Then I took the road that leads to Him,
> And became a slave at His gate;
> Then the duality disappeared
> And I became absorbed in Him.'

Jogendra Singh
September, 1938

THE INVOCATIONS

In the name of God,
Most Gracious,
Most Merciful.

O Thou Munificent One
Who art the bestower
Of all bounties,
O Thou wise One
Who overlookest our faults,

O Self-existent One
Who art beyond our comprehension,
O Thou omnipotent One
Who hast no equal in power and greatness.
Who art without a second:
O Thou merciful One
Who guidest stray souls to the right path,
Thou art truly our God.
Give purity to our minds,
Aspiration to our hearts,
Light to our eyes.

Out of Thy grace and bounty
Give us that which Thou deemest best.

O Lord, Out of Thy grace give faith and light to our hearts.
And with the medicine of truth and steadfastness cure the ills of our life.

I know not what to ask of Thee,
Thou art the Knower.
Give that which Thou deemest best.
O Lord! I have wasted my life,
Injured my soul,
And pleased the accursed Satan.
My being or not being is of little worth.
Accept my repentance and forgive my sins,
Take me from sorrow to happiness.

From the consequence of my past actions
And perils of the future
I see no way of escape.
O Lord! I am afraid of the evil within me.

Teach me how to save myself
from the snares of self;
Take me by the hand,
For without Thy mercy I have no refuge.
O God, may my brain reel with thoughts of Thee,
May my heart thrill with the mysteries of Thy grace,
May my tongue move only to utter
Thy praise.

I live only to do Thy will,
My lips move only in praise of Thee,
O Lord, whoever becometh aware of Thee
Casteth out all else other than Thee.
He who becometh aware of Thee
What use hath he for life,
For children, family or earthly things?

Whom Thou intoxicatest with Thy love
On him bestoweth Thou both the worlds.
But Thy mad devotee,
What use hath he for both the worlds?

O Lord, give me a heart
That I may pour it out in thanksgiving.
Give me life
That I may spend it
in working for the salvation of the world.

O Lord, give me that right discrimination
That the Lure of the world may cheat me no more.
Give me strength
That my faith suffer no eclipse.

O Lord, give me understanding,
That I stray not from the path.
Give me light
To avoid pitfalls.

O Lord, keep watch over me
That I stray not.
Keep me on the path of righteousness
That I escape from the pangs of repentance.

O Lord, judge me not by my actions,
Of Thy mercy, save me,
And make my humble efforts fruitful.

O Lord, give me a heart
Free from the flames of desire.
Give me a mind
Free from the waves of dissimulation.

O Lord, give me eyes
Which see nothing but Thy glory.
Give me a mind
That finds delight in Thy service.
Give me a soul
Drunk in the wine of Thy wisdom.

O Lord, to find Thee is my desire
But to comprehend Thee
Is beyond my strength.
Remembering Thee is solace
to my sorrowing heart,
Thoughts of Thee are my Constant Companions
I call upon Thee night and day.
The flame of Thy love glows
In the darkness of my night.

O Lord, he whom Thou killest doth not smell of blood,
And he whom Thou burnest doth not smell of smoke,
For he whom Thou burnest is happy in
The burning,
And he whom Thou killest, rejoiceth
In being killed.

O Lord, though the blue flower be poisonous
It is of Thy garden,
And if Abdullah be a sinner
He is of Thy people.

O Lord, when I think of Thy compassion
I feel like a crowned king;
When I think of my sins
I am as dust, nay, less than dust.

Life in my body pulsates only for Thee,
My heart beats in resignation to Thy will.
If on my dust a tuft of grass were
To grow
Every blade would tremble with my devotion
For Thee.

O Lord, every one desires to behold
Thee,
I desire
That Thou mayest cast a glance at me.

Let me not disgrace myself.
If Thy forgiveness awaits me in the end
Lower not the standard of forgiveness
Which Thou hast unfurled.

O Lord, if Thou sendest me to Hell
I raise no protest.
And if Thou takest me to Paradise,
I go there, but not of my own choice.

If in Hell I obtain union with Thee
What care I for those who dwell in Paradise?
And were I called to Heaven without Thee
The pleasures of Paradise would then
Be worse than the fires of Hell.

O Lord, prayer at Thy gate
Is a mere formality:
Thou knowest what Thy slave desires.

O Lord, better for me to be dust,
And my name effaced
From the records of the world,
Than that Thou forget me.

He knoweth all our good and evil
Nothing is hidden from Him.
He knoweth what is best medicine
To cure the pain,
And to rescue the fallen.
Be humble, for He exalteth the humble.

I am intoxicated with love of Thee
And need no fermented wine.
I am Thy bird
Free from need of seed
And safe from the snare of the fowler.
In the Ka'bah and in the Temple
Thou art the object of my search.
Else I am freed
From both these places of worship.

O Lord, when the fire of separation was burning me
Why didst Thou light the fire of Hell?

Lord, when Thou went hidden from me
The fever of life possessed me.
When Thou revealest Thyself
This fever of life departeth.
O Lord, other men are afraid of Thee
But I—I am afraid of myself,
From Thee flows good alone,
From me flows evil.

Each day I recall the day,
That is left behind.
Sorrowing over my misdeeds
The dread of my doings drives me to despair.
The thought of Thy mercy
Is the only solace of my heart.

Others fear what the morrow
May bring.
I am afraid of what happened yesterday.

O Lord, if Thou holdest me responsible for
My sins
I shall cling to Thee for Thy Grace.
I with my sin, am an insignificant atom.
Thy Gracc is resplendent as the Sun.

O Lord, out of regard for Thy name,
The qualities which are Thine,
Out of regard for Thy greatness,
Listen to my cry
For Thou alone canst redeem me.

O Lord, intoxicate me with the wine
Of Thy love.
Place the chains of Thy slavery on
My feet;
Make me empty of all but Thy love,
And in it destroy me and bring me
Back to life.
The hunger Thou has awakened, culminates
In fulfilment.

Make my body impervious to the fires
Of Hell;
Vouchsafe to me a vision of Thee in Heaven.
The spark Thou hast kindled make it
Everlasting.

I think of no other,
And in Thy love care for none else.
None has a place in my heart but Thee.
My heart has become Thy abode,
It has no place for another.

O Lord, Thou cherishest the helpless
And I am helpless,
Apply Thy balm to my bleeding heart
For Thou art the physician.
O Lord, I, a beggar, ask of Thee
More than what a thousand kings may ask of Thee;
Each one has something he needs to ask of Thee,
I have come to ask Thee to give me Thyself.

If words can establish a claim
I claim a crown.
But if deeds are wanted, I am as helpless as
The ant.

Urged by desire I wandered in the streets
Of good and evil,
I gained nothing except feeding the fire of desire.
As long as in me remains the breath of life
Help me, for Thou alone canst hear my prayer.

My friend, wisdom lies
In abandoning heedlessness,
In turning the heart away from the worldly objects,
And in gathering provision for the hereafter
Before departure from this earth.

Someone asked the Holy Prophet—
'What dost thou say concerning the things of the world?'
The Prophet said—'What can I say about them:
Things which are acquired with hard labour,
Preserved with perpetual watchfulness,
And left with regret.'

My friend, the world is not a place
For enjoyment,
But a place where humanity is on trial.
The world is a mere crossing
And not an abiding city of delight.
O mendicant, man is doomed to death
And has to leave the world.

Dost thou take the world for a friend
Or foe?
If thou holdest it a friend,
Know that it will not last.
If thou holdest it to be a foe, consume it,
So that it may not last.

Behold what thou art, and whence thou
Hast come.
Beware what thou doest and whither
Thou wouldest go,
If thou treadest the path of lust and longing
Thou shalt go without fruit and without good name.

My friend, put not thy reliance
On three things;
On heart, on time and on life.
The heart is easily tempted,
Time is always in a state of flux,
The sands of life run out.

My friend, make an effort,
That thou mayest become a man,
And gather treasures
Of feeling for others,
So that with the favour of saints
And by the blessings of waiting on them
Thy cheeks may grow pale,
And love of the world grow
Cold in thy heart.

If thou wishest to become a man
In the world,
In the path of religion
Learn to feel for others,
Night and day attend on holy men.
When thou hast become like dust
Of their feet
Thou shalt become a man.

O man, remember death at all times;
Renounce all discord and tyranny;
Deem what has not been done as done,
And what has been done as not done.

Watch vigilantly the state of
Thine own mind.
Love of God begins in
Harmlessness.

Know that the Prophet built an external Ka'bah
Of clay and water,
And an inner Ka'bah in life and heart.
The outer Ka'bah was built by Abraham,
The Holy;
The inner is sanctified by the glory of
God Himself.

On the path of God
Two places of worship mark the stages.
The material temple,
And the temple of the heart.
Make your best endeavour
To worship at the temple of the heart.

O mendicant, paradise is only an
Allurement;
The real objective is
the house of God Himself.

Fasting only means the saving of bread,
Formal prayer is the business
Of old men and women,
Pilgrimage is a pleasure of the world.
Conquer the heart,
Its subjection is conquest indeed.

If thou canst walk on water
Thou art no better than a straw.
It thou canst fly in air
Thou art no better than a fly.
Conquer thy heart
That thou mayest become somebody.

One man spends seventy years in learning
And fails to kindle the light.
Another, all his life learns nothing
But hears one word
And is consumed by that word.

On this path argument is of no avail;
Seek, and thou mayest find the truth.

Helpless in childhood,
Intoxicated in youth,
And decrepit in old age;
Then, O helpless one, when couldst thou
Worship God?

Alas! alas, for the master-craftsman's ways:
From the same iron he forges a horse-shoe
As well as a mirror for the Emperor.

My friend, see thine own faults;
The faults of others,
For thee they are not.
Make thy heart forgiving;
Nor sell thy soul for the fruits of the world.

It is wrong to consider oneself above all others
And to exalt one's self.
Learn from the pupil of thine eye
To see others, but to thyself be blind.

Know friend,
Human sorrow springs from three things:
To want before it is due,
To want more than the destined share,
To want for oneself
What belongs to others.

When Providence has provided thy share
Separately from others
Then why art thou jealous,
And hungering for that which is not for thee?

Desire for knowledge is the path
Of honour;
Desire for wealth, that of dishonour.

Wealth is the chain which slaves wear
Knowledge the kingly crown.

The path is narrow and beset by
Yawning chasms.
Woe to him who is heavily laden with sin
And walks without the light of faith.

He with whom virtue has become a habit,
Hath accomplished his work here,
and hereafter.

The law of life requires:

1. Sincerity to God.
2. Severity to self.
3. Justice to all people.
4. Service to elders.
5. Kindness to the young.
6. Generosity to the poor.
7. Good counsel to friends.
8. Forbearance with enemies.
9. Indifference to fools.
10. Respect to the learned.

Know that four things are symbols of
Ill luck:
Ingratitude in good fortune,
Impatience in ill fortune,
Discontent with what fate ordains,
Hesitation in serving fellow-men.

In this path, be a man
With a heart full of compassion.
Engage not in vain doing,
Make not thy home in the street of lust and desire.

If thou wouldst become a pilgrim on the path
Of love
The first condition is
That thou become as humble as dust
And ashes.

Remove 'A' from 'Murad' (desire) it becomes Murd (man);
He who renounceth desire becometh a man.

Know that he who desires the things of the
World
Is haunted by sorrow.
He who desires Heaven
Is a labourer working for wages.
But, he who desires God,
Is on the path of glory.

O thou who covetest the world
How long wilt thou follow the path of sorrow?
Even if thou seekest the pleasures of Heaven
Thy quest is on the wrong trail.
But if thou seekest God and receivest His seal,
Thou art victorious in both the worlds.

Know, that when thou learnest to lose thy self
Thou wilt reach thy Beloved.
There is no other secret to be revealed,
And more than this is not known to me.

Be humble and cultivate silence.
If thou hast received, rejoice,
And fill thyself with ecstasy
And it not, continue the demand.

Be a rose and not a thorn!
Be a friend and not an enemy!

To exalt the Beloved is to practise religion;
To exalt the self is to practise paganism.

If the seeker is worthy
Attainment is easy.

The company of a good friend
Is the light of the soul.
The company of an ungodly person
Is the poison of life.
A snake is preferable to a faithless friend.

Were I to abide in fire a hundred
Years
That scorching flame would be easier to bear
Than the company of Godless men;
Death is preferable to such company.

What is worship?
To realise reality.
What is the sacred law?
To do no evil.
What is reality?
Selflessness.

The heart enquired of the soul
What is the beginning of this business?
What its end, and what its fruit?
The soul answered:
The beginning of it is
the annihilation of self,
Its end faithfulness,
And its fruit immortality.
The heart asked what is annihilation?
What is faithfulness?
What is immortality?
The soul answered:
Freedom from self is annihilation;
Faithfulness is
Fulfilment of love;
Immortality is union of immortal
With mortal.

O Devotee, if thou lovest God truly
Why dost thou cast longing eyes
On things other than Him?

In this path the eye must cease to see,
And the car to hear.
Save unto Him, and about Him.
Be as dust on His path,
Even the kings of this earth
Make the dust of His feet
The balm of their eyes.

THE KNOWER AND THE KNOWN

He who knoweth
This body is of the earth
Gets rid of pride.

He who knoweth
God's law prevails
Is freed from sorrow.

He who knoweth
Each event is preordained
Plans no more.

He who knoweth
All that happens is from Him
Is freed from tribulation.

* * *

If thou lovest this world,
it will fail thee
If thou lovest God,
He will set thee free.

Work without fortitude
Undermines the roots of life.
Self-indulgent enjoyment
Only the worldly relish.

Be not courageous in sinning,
God metes out utter justice.
Fill not thyself with pride,
It is not pleasing to God.

Wert thou to know
The Creator,
The world could no more
Hold thee in thrall.

Suffering without resignation
Is like a burn without the balm.
Faith
That lacks reality
Is akin to faithlessness.

Blind obedience
Without the light of knowledge
Is utter waste of effort,
Like ploughing the sand.

If thou art freed
From the cage of this world
Soar into the Empyrean
And share the bliss of God.

Do not, O God, put out
This flickering lamp!
Cast not this heart afire with love for Thee
Into the furnace of desire!

Oh! God! Rend not
My patched-up sail.
Nor drive my broken bark,
From the river of knowledge!

Eyes that see an enemy
Are many thousands,
But the eye that sees a friend
Is one in a thousand.

Even a prison
Radiates happiness
If love for Thee
Fills the heart.

Blessed is enslavement
Which compels Thy service,
Thy bondsmen are happy
In their bondage.

There are two Ka'bahs:
The Ka'bah built on earth,
And the Ka'bah of the heart.

The first is the one that the feet
Of pilgrims frequent;
The other is the secret place
Which Seekers of Truth discover.

It is the former
Which fills the eyes of the faithful;
The other only the devotee finds
Under the eye of God Himself.

The pilgrimage to the earthly Ka'bah
Is a matter of formal discipline;
The finding of the Ka'bah of the heart
Depends on the grace of God.

At the one the pilgrims drink from the well of Zam-Zam;
The other unlocks its springs
To the welling up of sighs.

The earthly Ka'bah
Is guarded by the mountain of 'Irfat,
The temple of the heart
Is radiant with God's own light.

From the earthly Ka'bah
Stone idols were removed;
From the Ka'bah of the heart
Greed and desire are dethroned.

In this path
Anguished hearts bleed,
Like Jacob separated from his son
Like Majnun separated from his Laila.

If thou art a wanderer
From door to door
Close thine eyes
To the faults of others.

If thou doest
Some good deed
Let it not be known:
Better far, thy faults were revealed.

Oh! Friend! Keep away
From the ways of oppression;
To tyrannise His creation
Is to forget the Creator.

If thou desirest happiness
Choke then the springs of sorrow.
If thou wishest to attain thine object,
Labour for it without cease.

Renounce desire;
Overcome evil,
And rejoice not
In the misfortune of others.

By harsh words,
By ridicule or laughter,
Do not injure the feelings of others,
Refrain from indulgence in both.

Treat others
As thou wouldst be treated.
What thou likest not for thyself
Dispense not to others.

O! Man of firm Faith
Do good and earn the reward.
Let not ingratitude
Enter thy heart.

If thou art a wanderer
In search of Truth
Betray not thy secret
To the outer world.

Why remain a bondsman
Of greed, or mere speculator
On the mysteries of life.
Devotion alone can fulfil thy need.

Be not proud of wealth
'Tis but temporarily lent.
Treasure, more than aught else,
The gift of health.

O God! Fill me with Thy Grace
So that the passions of the body
Assail my mind no more!

Help me, O God!
For none else can
Bestow Thy gifts;
Thou art the only Giver.

I am aware
Of my own unworthiness,
But I am certain
Of Thy boundless grace.

* * *

Regard not thyself
With thine own eye
Lest it may bring misfortune
By magnifying the self.

The evil eye of another
Can be averted,
There is no escape
From the evil of one's own.

Satan saw himself
With his own eye, created out of fire,
He looked down on Adam
Created out of earth.

Satan who looked at himself,
With his own eye, was condemned for ever.
Adam, on whom he cast an evil eye,
Craved forgiveness and was redeemed.

'Tis better to be
Humble as the earth
Rather than steeped
In overweening self-conceit.

When Mansur was imprisoned
For proclaiming oneness with God,
His friend Shibli asked him
'What is this love?'

'Come to-morrow
For answer,' he said.
Shibli obeyed and found Mansur
Facing the gallows.

Mansur looked at him
And said, 'Read the answer:
Love begins in absorbing the "I"
And ends thus':

'Its noose tightens
To squeeze out the self
Then comes the test of the Cross.
Stay it thou apprehendest the secret, otherwise go.'

Men are like addicts of drink,
Unaware of their own state.
The wise are wide-awake,
Having cast out the spell.

Wealthy men are narrow-hearted,
Others, discontented for all time,
Lament their misfortunes
Real and imagined.

The emancipated are freed
From bonds of being, and non-being:
They have broken the cage
And found their freedom.

They have emptied
The cup of desire;
They strive no more
For worldly greatness.

Freed from joy and sorrow
They have found their true self;
They dwell for ever more
In the wondrous realm of God.

If a lame dog
Finds admission at Thy gate,
And the weary are refreshed by Thy sight
No reason have I for despair.

WORDS OF WISDOM

O! thou wanderer in the wilderness of the world
See the graveyards that lie about thee.
Realise the truth, that life passes,
And be not heedless, as drunkards are.

Under tomb-stones and in mausoleums sleep
Thousands that blossomed like the rose,
And wasted precious days
In mad pursuit of pleasure.

They too were unwearying
Planning for Profit and Pastime,
And attainment of perpetual enjoyment,
Completely forgetful of the future.

They too ardently desired
Greatness and Jewelled Diadems;
They feasted on dainty dishes
And drank from goblets of silver and of gold.

They nursed in the soil of their hearts
The seed of Earthly pleasures,
Gathering in their Earthly homes
All the treasures of the Earth.

Suddenly they were called upon
To drink from the hands of Azrael*
Sherbet of mortality, and enter
The gate of Death.

* Azrael, the Angel of Death.

They were like bankrupt Bankers
Leaving their treasures behind
Gathered from the fields of sufferings
Their only gain—a sorrowing soul.

Friends, remember always
That all that lives must die;
Therefore prepare for the future,
Otherwise, Hell is your assured portion.

O, ye heedless young men!
O, ye ignorant old men, who have learnt nothing!
Are ye mad not to realise
The truth of life?

In days of old,
Before your time,
I too like you, strode the carpeted earth
As if it was mine for ever.

I too slept on soft beds,
And stepped on rugs of velvet;
I too held gorgeous banquets,
And indulged in pleasure

Before I became aware of the peril;
The ruin that awaited me,
The loss of love and affection,
The waste of gold and wealth.

The cup of life was empty;
I was marched out
Bringing nothing from the world,
Not even love and loyalty of friends.

My acts and deeds and weary work
Gathered for me no grace;
From friends and family came no help;
My hoarded wealth afforded no relief.

Now I am overwhelmed with shame
How to face the day of Judgment.
Friendless and forlorn
I carry nothing with me.

No visitors throng the portals of the grave;
No callers come for a pleasant talk;
No sound disturbs the silence;
My body is turning into a handful of dust.

Pleasures of the world
Are things of the past;
My flesh and skin
Are an offering to the worms.

When the opportunity was mine
I had no discrimination
To seek reality from the unreal.
I was wrapped in forgetfulness—even as you.

Here I lie under Earth
My teeth are all scattered;
Earth is eating into my limbs,
Taking them back to herself.

My home is in ruins;
The fruits of my labour are swallowed up
My children find no place in my house;
Another sleeps on my bed.

I now shed tears of repentance,
And lament over my misdeeds.
Take warning from me
And work while there is still time.

The bird of the soul will take wing
And leave the body untenanted.
Grass will grow over the grave,
And perchance a flower unfold.

PART TWO

ANSARI'S PRAYERS AND COUNSELS

From *Sufism: An Account of Mystics of Islam*

Translated by
Arthur John Arberry

Thou, Whose breath is sweetest perfume to the spent and anguished heart,
Thy remembrance to Thy lovers bringeth ease for every smart.
Multitudes like Moses, reeling, cry to earth's remotest place:
Give me sight, O Lord![*] they clamour, seeking to behold Thy face.
Multitudes no man has numbered, lovers, and afflicted all,
Stumbling on the way of anguish, 'Allah, Allah!' loudly call.

---

* These words are a quotation from the *Qur'an*, S. vii 139. The story is, that during the sojourn of the Children of Israel in the wilderness, after their flight from Egypt, Moses on one occasion said to God, 'O Lord, show Thyself to me, that I may look upon Thee.' God replied, 'Thou shalt not see Me; but look towards the mountain, and if it abide firm in its place, then shalt thou see Me.' Moses looked, and the mountain crumbled into dust; and Moses fell swooning. The story is frequently on the lips of the Muslim mystics as an example of the spiritual vision of God.

And the fire of separation sears the heart and burns the breast,
And their eyes are wet with weeping for a love that gives not rest.
'Poverty's my pride!'* Thy lovers raise to heav'n their battle-cry,
Gladly meeting men's derision, letting all the world go by.
Such a fire of passion's potion Pir-i-Ansar† quaffing feels
That distraught, like Leylah's lover,‡ through a ruined world he reels.

---

* A well-known saying, which in the Arabic takes point from the play on words between *fakhr* (pride) and *faqr* (poverty).

† This is the *takhallus* or poetical *nom-de-plume* adopted by Ansari, after the fashion of all the Persian poets. Pir (literally 'old man') is the usual designation of the 'holy man' in Persian mystical literature, and is thus an exact rendering of its Arabic counterpart '*sheykh*'.

‡ Leylah's lover, Manjnun or 'madman', was a poet of the tribe of Amir, by name Qeys. His sin was, that he celebrated the beauty of Leylah, and his love for her, so bringing shame upon her according to the strict desert rule of his day. Leylah's subsequent refusal to marry him, and the story of his distracted wandering, and of the tragic death of both Leylah and Qeys, are celebrated in Islamic literature and art.

O Generous, Who bounty givest!
O wise, Who sins forgivest!
O Eternal, Who to our senses comest not near!
O One, Who art in essence and qualities without peer!
O Powerful, Who of Godhead worthy art!
O Creator, Who showest the way to every erring heart!

To my soul give Thou of Thy own spotlessness,
And to my eyes of Thy own luminousness:
And unto us, of Thy bounty and goodness, whatever may be best,
Make Thou that Thy bequest.

O Lord, in mercy grant my soul to live,
And patience grant, that hurt I may not grieve:
How shall I know what thing is best to seek?
Thou only knowest: what Thou knowest, give.

O God, accept my plea, and to my faults indulgent be.
O God, all my days I have spent in vanity, and against my own body have I wrought iniquity.
O God, before lies danger, and behind path have I none to go:
Take Thou my hand, for beside Thy bounty refuge none I know.

O God, I tremble for mine iniquity:
For Thine own Self's sake do Thou pardon me.
O God, bring not to the dust our faith's firm foundations,
And turn not to a wilderness the garden of our aspirations.
O God, before Thy love both worlds hold we in disdain,
And about our bodies we have wrapped the robe of pain,
And the veil of pardon we have rent in twain.

O God, upon whomsoever Thou hast set the seal of Thy affection,
The barn of his existence Thou hast swept clean on the wind of utter destruction.
O God, without Thee no hope is there of felicity,
And apart from Thee no means is there of liberty.
O God, if any man Thee would know,
All other things but Thee away he must throw.

What recks he for his life, who Thee hath known?
What cares he for his wife, his child, his own?
Thou firest him, and giv'st him all that is:
What boots him all, who craves for Thee alone?

O God, give us a heart, that in Thy service our lives we may stake;
And give us a soul, that whatever thing we do, we may do it for Heaven's sake.
O God, give us to taste of affliction, lest in ease our watchfulness depart;
And give us contentment, lest cupidity possess our heart.
O God, support Thou me, for in myself I have no security;
And accept my plea, for I have no means to flee.

O God, say not, 'What hast thou brought,'
Lest I hide my face;
And ask not of me, 'What hast thou wrought?'
Lest it turn to my disgrace.

O God, give us Thy evidence,
That we may leave this world without complaint;
And guard us in Thy providence,
That in the world to come we may not faint.

O God, watch over us, lest confusion break us;
And lead us on our way, lest bewilderment overtake us.

O God, do Thou bless,
For this is not given to any man;
And do Thou caress,
For this no other can.

O God, give us a heart, that it may in Thy obedience increase;
And help us to obey, that we may come to Paradise and peace.
O God, give us a knowledge that hath in it no fire of cupidity;
And give us a practice that hath in it no water of hypocrisy.

O God, give us an eye that knows
But masterhood in Thee;
And give us a heart that owes
But servanthood to Thee.

O God, give me a spirit to carry in my ear the ring
of Thy mastery;
And give me a soul to turn to honey the sting
of Thy afflicting me.

O God, to find Thee we desire:
To understand Thee, to this we have not strength to aspire.
O God, whomsoever Thou slayest, him do Thou heal;
And whomsoever Abdullah slays, that do Thou conceal.*

O God, whom Thou hast slain, he is content;
And whomsoever Thou hast burnt, he maketh merriment.

O God, when we are disobedient, Thy friend Muhammad
is sorrowful thereat, and Thy enemy Iblis is glad;
And at the Resurrection, if Thou dost punish, Thy friend
will be sore troubled thereat, and Thy enemy glad.

---

* God's 'slaying' is, of course, the affliction which He causes the mystic to experience; and Abdullah's (that is, the author's) 'slaying' refers in a general sense to all his sins.

O God, give not two joys to Thy enemy, and give not two sorrows to the heart of Thy friend.
O God, if once Thou sayest to me, 'My servant,' thereafter beyond the empyrean will ascend my laughter.
O God, though succory is bitter, yet in the garden with the rose it blends;
And though Abdullah be a sinner, yet is he among Thy friends.

My heart might never beat, save pleasing Thee,
And for Thy sake my spirit lives in me:
When on my mounded grave the grass grows high,
Each scented blade shall breath fidelity.

O God, Thou saidst, 'Do this,' and didst not let me;
Thou badest, 'Do this not,' and didst permit me.*
O God, do not depose the sign which Thou dost raise:
And since Thou wilt at last grant pardon, do not Thou at first abase.

---

* The author here proposes the paradox of man's free-will. God gave men liberty to determine their own conduct, and also commanded them to obey Him. This very gift of free-will, however, must inevitably lead to their damnation.

O God, of what avail is it the obedient to forgive,
Or what worth is there in bounty which all do not receive?

O Lord, I sin: where is Thy loving glance?
My heart is black: where is Thy radiance?
If Paradise is by obedience bought,
Where lies Thy bounty, Thy munificence?

O God, whatever man Thou wouldst overcast,
Among the dervishes him do Thou cast.*
O God, though Paradise is all light and gladness,
To those who see Thee not it is all sorrow and sadness.

O God, Thy beauty only lives: the rest is ugliness;
The pious are the hirelings of eternal bliss.†
O God, would that Abdullah but dust had been,
That of his name the register of life might be wiped clean.

---

* 'Overcast' is here used in the familiar mystical sense of 'abasement'. The dervishes (Persian equivalent of the Arabic *faqir* or fakir) are the afflicted of God, and outcast by men.

† Pious men obey God only in the hope of winning a place in Paradise: therefore they may be said to 'hire' their good deeds to Paradise. True service is service for God's sake only, without thought of reward. So Rabi'ah, the famous woman-mystic, is reported to have prayed: 'O God! if I worship Thee in fear of Hell, burn me in Hell; and if I worship Thee in hope of Paradise, exclude me from Paradise; but if I worship Thee for Thine own sake, withhold not Thine everlasting beauty!' (Nicholson, *The Mystics of Islam*, p. 115).

Small profit was my coming yesterday:
Today life's market's not more thronged or gay.
Tomorrow I shall go unknowing hence;
Far better were it to have stayed away.

O God, Abu Jahl* from the Ka'bah comes, Abraham from the idol-shrine:
Thy providence doth order all things; what remains is but a vain pretence.
O God, there is indeed light in obedience,
But the ruling of affairs is in Thy providence.

When rules God's providence, iniquity
At last is proven purest piety,
Oppression marks the ruler's proper awe,
And church and mosque both house Divinity.

---

* Abu Jahl was one of Muḥammad's most implacable enemies: the Commentators on the *Qur'an* aver that it is to him that Surah xcvi refers in the words 'What thinkest thou of him that holdeth back a servant (of God) when he prayeth?' In Muslim religious literature he is chosen as the prototype of wilful disbelief, a distinction which his nickname, 'father of ignorance,' eloquently illustrates. Abraham is held by Muslims to have been the builder of the Ka'bah at Mecca, the sacred shrine in which the famous 'Black Stone' is preserved. Our author in this sentence implies that with God all things are possible, and that on His grace alone depends man's salvation. The quatrain which follows illustrates the same point.

O God, in gold and silver the rich take pride:
The poor resign themselves to *We do decide**
O God, all other men are drunk with wine: the wine-
bearer is my fever.
Their drunkenness lasts but a night: mine abides for ever.

Thou art my wine: I ask no greater bliss.
Thou art my captor: other cage none is.
In idol-shrine and Ka'bah Thee I seek,
Else am I free of that abode and this.

---

* This is a quotation from *Qur'an*, xliii, 31.

O God, my weakness I confess,
And I myself am a witness to my helplessness.
O God, Thine only is the Will:
What then shall I will?

O God, since Thou hast kindled the fire of separation,
What need hadst Thou to light the furnace of damnation?
O God, extinguish not this lamp by Thee made bright,
And consume not this heart by Thee set alight:
Rend not this veil by Thy hand sewn,
And banish not this slave who hath learnt all from Thee
alone.

O God, every foot of scorn Thou settest on Abdullah's face,
And every heart by anguish worn Thou raisest to
Abdullah's place.

O God, when I could accomplish so,
I did not know:
And when I knew,
Then I could not do.

O God, by the sanctity of the Name that is Thine,
And by the sanctity of Thy qualities divine!
As Thou art able, do Thou shelter me.

O God, make Thou complete the foretaste which Thou hast given,
And make perpetual this lightning-flash whereby my soul Thou hast riven.

More than a thousand monarchs dare aspire
To dream, my hope, a beggar's Lord, mounts higher.
Let other men their fond ambitions tell:
Lo, I have come from Thee, and Thee desire!

O my friend, know that this world is a place where life is but a little measure,
A city given up to pleasure.
Its sting inflicts a wound beyond medicament's resource,
And from it Ibrahim the son of Adham sought divorce.*
It is a house of lawlessness and little peace,
And from it Junayd Baghdadi† sought release.

It is a potion that consumes the soul, so bitter is its flavour:
Shaqiq of Balkh‡ turned from it in disfavour.
Its sum is loss and evil reputation:
Ba Yazid Bistami fled from it with execration.§
It is a cloister for self-worshippers, who for God have no care:

---

* Ibrahim b. Adham was a prince of Balkh living in the latter half of the 8th century CE. The story of his conversion while hunting is well known (see Nicholson, *Literary History of the Arabs*, p. 232).

† Juneyd of Baghdad, who died in 909, and styled by the Arabs the 'Sheykh of Sheykhs' is the most celebrated exponent of the 'sober' type of mysticism. His *Rasa'il*, consisting of letters to his contemporaries, together with short tracts on various mystical subjects, have fortunately survived. A specimen of his letters is given in JRAS 1935, PP. 499-507.

‡ Shaqiq of Balkh was a well-known mystic of the period following Ibrahim b. Adham. He is reported to have been particularly concerned to stress the virtue of *tawakkul* (absolute trust in God).

§ Ba Yazid, or Abu Yazid, of Bistam, was a contemporary and teacher of Juneyd (he died in 874). He is the greatest exponent of 'intoxicated' mysticism, and some of his ecstatic sayings, such as Subhani ('Glory be to me!'), were quoted by the opponents of Şufism as patent examples of atheism, but by the Sufis themselves as illustrating the state of *fana* or complete passing away from self into God.

It was rejected by Abu Sa'id the son of Abu'l-Kheyr.*
Pious men decline it:
Sinners to the highest place assign it.

He is abased who seeketh it,
And his tongue to find excuse hath little wit.
These words bear warning to such as will give ear:
Say, the goods of this world are but little cheer.†

* Abu Sa'id (d. 1049) was a distinguished poet as well as being a noted mystic. His biography, by Muhammad b. Al-Munawwar, has been published. For examples of his quatrains, see Browne, *Literary History of Persia*, II, pp. 264-7.

† A quotation from *Qur'an*, iv. 79.

O my friend, behold yon cemetery, and see
How many tombs and graves there be;
How many hundred thousand delicate ones there sleep
in slumber deep.

Much toiled they every one and strove,
And feverishly burned with barren hope and selfish love,
And shining garments jewel-sprinkled wove.
Jars of gold and silver fashioned they,
And from the people profit bore away,
Much trickery revealing,
And great moneys stealing;

But, at the end, with a full regretful sigh,
They lay them down to die.
Their treasuries they filled,
And in their hearts well-tilled
Planted the seed
Of lustful greed:
But, at the last,
From all these things they passed.

So burdened, suddenly,
At the door of death they sank,
And there the cup of destiny
They drank.

O my friend, ponder well thy dissolution,
And get thee betimes thine absolution;
Or, know it full well,
Thou shalt in torment dwell.

Know that thy friends in earth to implore thee are seeking;
The wretched state in which they are for them is speaking:

'O young men indolent!
O old men impotent!

'Haply ye are mad, that ye have not seen how that we in earth and blood are sleeping,
Our faces in the death-shroud obscurely keeping:
So at our fated time we die,
And in a week forgotten lie.

'We, too, before you came knew happiness,
And clutched the evanescent world with joy and eagerness:
We drank the milk of earthly pleasure,
But at the last knew death's appointed measure.

'We saw no security in living:
After so vain striving
We saw ourselves on the wind of annihilation scattered,
And to the earth in dire affliction battered.

'Our friends and families showed us no compassion,
Our wealth and winnings profited us not in any fashion.

'But we were satisfied with this regret,
Did not await us resurrection yet.

'Now have we neither pillow nor pallet,
Neither garment nor wallet:
No strength have we to cry out,
No power left to speak or shout,
Helpless, cast out.

‘Our portion of this world is banishment:
Our flesh, our skin for worms is nourishment.

‘Time was, when we had power, when our treasury was not yet spent,
We gave but little heed,
And of wisdom found no need:
But presently our souls were rent with strife,
And so we yielded up our life.

‘Now, if ye be not quite delirious,
Look once more on us.

‘Now mourn we all
And we let fall
The tear of vain regret, and for ourselves make funeral.

‘Our present state is unutterable,
And for our past misdeeds we are sorrowful.

‘Friends, turn your gaze on us,
And mark our state calamitous.

‘Forgotten are our names,
Vanished our fleshly frames;
Our bones are putrefied,
Our flesh is liquified;
Our hoarded wealth scattered,
Our loved abodes shattered.

‘Of our bed another now is lord;
Our children are driven from their board;
Our cheek with mud is spattered,
Our teeth are scattered;
Our tongue is stilled;
Our mouth with dust is filled.

'Our spirit's bird is flown,
And from our dust is sorrow's verdure grown.
'We lie in the dark earth deep:
Ye in forgetfulness sleep.'

O my friend, the sign of wisdom is this, that in thy heart this world thou shouldst forsake,
And from the sleep of heedlessness awake,
Ere from this world departure taking,
Provision for thy heavenly dwelling making.

If thy path is wrapped in shadow,
Lo, here is light:
Give no thought to far tomorrows,
Take joy tonight.

All who dwell on earth must perish:[*]
This sure decree
Glory turns to dust, and pleasure
To misery.

---

* A quotation from *Qur'an*, lv. 26.

In thy narrow coffin sleeping
For ever lie:
Though of ivory thy throne was,
So thou must die.

Now at last thou art at leisure
The truth to know;
Now at last what most thou lackest
The tomb will show.

Disobedience hath corrupted
Thy pure estate:
Now let abstinence restore thee
Immaculate.

Put to flight corruption's shadow
With penitence,
And thy soul shall spread tomorrow
New radiance.

Pir-i-Ansar sin hath broken
This bleeding heart:
Haply God's eternal bounty
Will ease thy smart.

O men of might!
In the market-place ye are a delight,
But in the mosque ye are far from sight:
In sin ye dwell both day and night;
Your worldly state is prosperous, but your spiritual state is ruined quite.

In youth ye have no shame,
And in old age feel no blame.

Your life is wasted in misuse,
Yet seek ye not to find excuse.

Death privily awaits you, and a dwelling beneath the sod:
Then shall ye return to God.

For earthly sorrows your hearts do bleed:
The wrath to come ye do not heed.

Beware, my spirit, thy Creator's wrath:
Perils beset thy path.
Break through the sleep of heedlessness, and hear
My counsel wise and clear.

Mark yonder place, where men at last abide
Like offal, cast aside:
Behold how sped annihilation's dart
And pierced each bucklered heart.

Full many a king, whose monuments adorn
The world, here lies in scorn;
Full many a sweet delight held heart in thrall,
But proved to spirit gall.

This fleeting world is but a ferry-way:
The wise man will not stay.
Since death O Pir-i-Ansar, lies ahead,
Stride on with quickened tread.

Know that this world is but a hostelry, to stay, and then pass by;
And know that man is born to die.

The well is lost today,
And narrow is the way;

And woe to him who putteth out faith's flame,
And binds upon himself the load of sin and shame.

Drive not the poor man from thy door at night:
His loud complaint will mount to heaven's height.
Fearest thou not the full repentant sigh
Which from his seared heart arrow-like doth fly?
Beware the magic of that dart, whose pace
Hath power to pierce the mountain's rocky face!
If in the midnight God's name he implores,
A thousand others drive him from their doors.
A thousand daggers poison-tipped flash out
To fight his cause who unto God doth shout:
Behold, the poor man's burning sighs prevail
To melt like wax a thousand coats-of-mail.
Think not to wanton with impunity:
As thou hast dealt, so time shall deal with thee.
Strike not anew the lacerated soul;
The day of reckoning will take full toll:
Though the wronged suppliant murmurs not, know well
He Who marks all will cast thee into Hell.
Weep not, Abdullah, for the harsh man's sin:
Though all-reject thee, God will take thee in.

O my friend, bestir thyself, and be a man:
Get thee experience, and suffer whilst thou can;

That through the benedictions of the poor, and the blessings of their visitations, thy face may be made bright,
And the goods of this world become mean in thy sight.

Wouldst thou attain the fullness of thy span?
Wouldst thou endure all that the spirit can?
Then day and night get thee about with men:
Being with men, thou wilt become a man.*

Know that God Most High has built an outward Ka'bah out of mud and stone,
And fashioned an inward Ka'bah of heart and soul alone.

The outward Ka'bah Abraham did build,
The inward Ka'bah was as the Lord Almighty willed.

* A man, that is, of God.

The outward Ka'bah is for faithful eyes a spectacle,
The inward Ka'bah is seen by God the Merciful.

Two Ka'bahs are there on the heavenly road:
One outward is, and one the heart's abode.
So, if thou canst, to hearts make pilgrimage:
One heart is worth a thousand shrines of God.*

O my friend, this world is an abode for resting,
Nay rather, it is a place of testing.

One man's desire thereof is Paradise, another's is the Friend:
Let me be his ransom, who makes God his end!

Who seeks this world, suffers grief;
Who seeks the world to come, holds it in fief;†
Who seeks his master, his is joy beyond belief.

---

* The Tradition runs, 'Whoso knows himself, has known his Lord,' and self-examination is the foundation of all mysticism.

† For he is a 'hireling' of Heaven; see p. 376, n. 2.

Know, that when thou hast broken selfhood's chain,
Then thou wilt the friend attain.

No signpost marks this way:
The manner of this mystery no tongue can say.

Intoxicated be, but do not shout;
Broken, and not cry out:
The whole pitcher goes in hand, the broken pitcher is on shoulder borne about.

If thou hast, celebrate:
If thou hast not, supplicate.

Be a rose, and not a thorn:
Be a friend, and not an alien born.

To approve thy host is faithfulness:
To make false boast is unbelief, no less.

Neighbour right,
Labour light.

Though I must lie in Hell a century,
Yet would that burning blaze not trouble me.
But give me not a traitor for a friend:
Far worse than death is evil company.

If on this path the gnostic* seeks but Paradise and its seductive joys,†
The purity of his gnosis that quest destroys;
And if the dervish seeks not god seeking of god,
Never will god grant him his assenting nod.

If thou wilt listen to thy inward heart,
Full many a mystery it doth impart:
If self denying thou art dead to self,
Hear now the wondrous tidings, 'God thou art!'‡

---

* The gnostic is, in Sufi language, the man who possesses *ma'rifah* or gnosis, the spiritual knowledge of God.

† Literally, 'houris,' the 'dark-eyed maidens' of Paradise.

‡ Through *fana* (see p. 378, n. 4) the mystic passes away from his own selfhood, and becomes absorbed in the all-pervading Selfhood of God.

O dervish, Paradise is but a plea:
Thy proper quest the master of the house must be.
True service is not fasting and supplication:
True service is a contrite heart and resignation.

In god's service eagerness of heart reveal,
And all thy faults conceal
Of thy own shortcomings be aware,
The faults of others spare.

Whoever takes ten qualities to be his text*
Acquires advantage in this world and the next:
Towards god, truthfulness; towards men, justice; towards self,
harshness; towards his betters, civility; towards children,
gentleness; towards the poor, generosity; towards friends,
giving good counsel; towards enemies, clemency; towards
fools, silence; towards the wise, humility.

* Literally, 'watchword.'

The Lord of the World* was asked: 'What sayest thou concerning this present world?'
He replied: 'What shall I say of a thing which
men with labour get
retain with sweat,
And leave with regret?'

O my friend, count this life a capital to gain,
And seek from self in service refuge to obtain
Death is the universal bane.
Give not thy soul its lust,
And in an ignorant man put not thy trust.

Seek help of god in every affair
Of friend and enemy alike beware.
Not having seen or heard, speak not thy mind:
Be conscious of thy faults, to other men's be blind.

---

* Sc. the Prophet.

On God's path seek not liberty to win,
And look not harshly on another's sin.
God knows the secret of each human heart
Think not to make thyself His peer therein.

Twist not the truth; answer not in haste; until men ask thee, do not speak,
and go not forth, unless they seek.
Sell not what men will not buy.
Take not up again what thou hast once set down.
Reckon not as done what is not done.
Make not thy soul a plaything of the devil.
In secret be a better man than publicly.
Eat no man's bread, but grudge not thine to any man.
Of thy soul's commands beware.
Though thy enemy be weak, do not despise him.
Make not a journey with a fool.
Reckon thy little better than other men's much.

Grieve not to no purpose: know that God's friendship rests in making little trouble.
Know that happiness in this world and the next is won by the companionship of those who know.

Associate not with men who do not know.
Make generosity thy habit, and take pride in poverty.
Acquiesce in God's decree: be of good manners, and make little trouble.

Do not unto others what thou wouldst not do unto thyself.
If thou desirest happiness, endure pain.
If thou wouldst attain joy, be patient, and make humility thy habit and boast not of thyself.

It is a sin, to hold oneself too high,
To please oneself, and others to deny.
The eye sees all, itself it cannot see:
Learn wisdom from the parable of the eye.*

---

* The following rendering of this quatrain is by E. G. Browne:
'Great shame it is to deem of high degree
Thyself, or over others reckon thee:
Strive to be like the pupil of thine eye---
To see all else, but not thyself to see.'

Do good, and thou wilt have thy recompense.
Give pain to no man with an unkind word.
Be not a slave to greed, and be not led away by heedlessness.

Know that possessions are but a loan: count good health for a gain.
Know that a thousand friends are little worth, and that single enemy can do great hurt.

Take not a loan from a man with a new purse.
Give respect to an ancient house, but do not boast of power.
Keep thyself far from bigotry.
Say of a man in secret only what thou canst say to his face.
Rail not against the suppliant, and make not the mendicant despair.

Know that thy brother Muslim's need is a grave affair.
Talk not of the good which thou hast done, and speak not ill of any man.
Cause men to hope in thee, and show not gladness at any man's misfortune.
Do injury to no man, and look for sincerity only in the noble man.

O my friend, know that sorrow comes to a man from three things:
He wishes for days departed irrevocably,
For a greater portion from destiny,
And for another man's patrimony.
Since one man's bread is different from another's,
Why concern thyself about thy brother's?
Guard thy tongue, but not thy wealth:
Watch not the world, but watch thy spirit's health.
Alas, for those who spend their night in sleep,
Their day lost in delusion deep,
Not knowing that from god they are far away,
And tomorrow in the dust will lay.

My life, alas, is spent in worthless ways;
Vain penitence my streaming cheek displays.
Drunken by day, and drowned in sleep at night,
Remorse at dawn-so pass the precious days.

In childhood thou art powerless;
Thy youth is spent in drunkenness;
In age thou all too languid art:
When wilt thou take god's service to thy heart?

Thy faith is but a word, a barren token:
A hundred idols stand, not one is broken.
Tonight brings revelry, remorse tomorrow:
Faith is not proved, when 'God is Great' is spoken.*

* To say '*Allah Akbar*' ('God is Greater'), the Islamic formula of faith, is not enough to prove true belief. If the hundred 'idols' (of personal desire and sinfulness) are still not overthrown, then the worshipper still has the greater part of the journey to make.

A fine place is this world, I trow!
Wherever thou dost go, men ask thee, 'Who art thou?'
If thou comest, open stands the gate:
And if thou comest not, no man is disconsolate.
If this world thou lovest, give it not away, that it may stay with thee;
But if thou hatest it, devour it, that it may vanish utterly.
Yesterday is gone, and will not come again:
Tomorrow may not come, to trust in it is vain.
Count today for a gain:
It will not long remain.

O my friend, be a man, if thou wouldst go upon this way:
Let anguish ever in thy spirit stay.
Do naught indiscreet,
And stand not in vile passion's street.

If thou wouldst leave thy empty lusts, and know
What will release thee from this earthly woe,
Consider who thou art, whence thou hast come,
What here thou dost, and whither thou must go.

Give not thy heart to men, or thou wilt have but little peace:
Yield thy heart to God, and thou shalt find release.
All things that fill this world for man's delight were made,
But all his happiness is on God's service stayed.

Every man, be he a door-keeper or a king,
Must unto God Almighty service bring.
In God's sight he must make his soul's ablution,
If he would taste the water of absolution.

God said: 'I made creation, that men might call Me Artisan:
Then I destroyed it, that they might know I have not need of any man.

To whomsoever I gave leave to be,
I gave him life that he might worship Me.'

O dervish, worship God with patience, till thy earthly labour endeth,
And god's providence descendeth;
Till god's throne shineth clear,
And the dawn of union draweth near:
Then cometh thy supreme felicity,
Then god's eternal beauty thou shalt see.

ALSO IN SPEAKING TIGER CLASSICS

THE ANT WHO SWALLOWED THE SUN

The Abhangs of the Marathi Women Saints

Translated by NEELA BHAGWAT and JERRY PINTO

One colour now, one colour, You and me, one colour.
I look at You, Panduranga, one look, no You, no me.

The Bhakti movement, which began around the 6th century, transformed Indian thought in fundamental ways. It took seed in Maharashtra in the early 13th century in the form of the Warkari movement. With unmatched passion and eloquence, the Warkari saint-poets spread the message of universal humanism combining it with a deep devotion towards Vitthal. *The Ant Who Swallowed the Sun* is a collection of translations of abhangs by ten prominent and lesser- known Marathi women-saints belonging to this movement.

These women came from diverse backgrounds: Muktabai was Saint Dynaneshwar's sister; Janabai was Saint Namdev's maid, Rajai his wife and Gonai his mother; Bahinabai was a brahmin trapped in a difficult marriage; Kanhopatra, a sex-worker; Soyarabai and Nirmala were from lower castes; and not much is known about Bhagu and Vatsara. At a time when women hardly had any autonomy, each claimed Vitthal as their own, addressing him variously as the divine, the lover or the friend. Their abhangs are not just expressions of devotion but offer a scathing criticism of patriarchy and caste hierarchies. With Neela Bhagwat and Jerry Pinto's pitch-perfect translations, *The Ant Who Swallowed the Sun* is an important addition to Bhakti literature, as well as a delight for poetry lovers.

ALSO IN SPEAKING TIGER CLASSICS

GOD IS DEAD, THERE IS NO GOD

The Vachanas of Allama Prabhu

Translated by Manu V. Devadevan

Twelfth-century saint-poet Allama Prabhu, along with Basavanna and Akka Mahadevi, was a founder of the Virashaiva or Lingayat movement in Karnataka. During a period of intense religious ferment, these Sharanas—protégés of Shiva—aimed to dismantle religious hierarchy and bigotry. They rebelled against exploitation based on class, caste and gender. And the form of expression they chose was the vachana—poetic compositions in everyday Kannada, which shook 12th-century Karnataka out of slumber. Today, with their focus on devotion towards Shiva through love, labour and dedication, they form an integral part of the Bhakti tradition as well as India's cultural heritage.

The vachanas of Allama Prabhu symbolize his journey of freeing himself from worldly attachments and bondages. From gazing at Shiva from a distance, to uniting with Him, to declaring He doesn't exist and to finally realizing that He should be understood as a dynamic void: Allama covers a wide arc in his quest for spiritual enlightenment. Rooted firmly in the idea of experiential reality, his vachanas are passionate and filled with yearning; critical and brazen. Translated with great skill and fluidity by Manu Devadevan, *God Is Dead, There Is No God* is a treat for modern-day seekers as well as poetry lovers.

